From Pain

to

Poetic Justice

From Pain to Poetic Justice

Reflections in Poetry

D'onte J. Carroll

Kingdom Living Publishing
Fort Washington, MD

Copyright © 2012 D'onte J. Carroll

All rights reserved under International Copyright Law. No part of this book may be reproduced or transmitted in any form or by any means without written permission of the Publisher, except for the inclusion of brief quotations in a review.

Cover concept and graphic by Denzel Williams, Destined Designs, Washington, DC
www.destined-designs.com

Cover design by Tamika Hayden, TLH Designs, Chicago, IL
www.tlhdesigns.com

Published by
Kingdom Living Publishing
10905 Livingston Road
Fort Washington, MD 20744

Printed in the United States of America.
ISBN 978-0-9799798-3-5

Acknowledgments

First and foremost, I want to thank God for giving me the ability, the gift and anointing to write.

To my Wife, Abronda, thank you for spiritually covering me in prayer, believing in me, putting up with me and being my best friend. I thank you for your obedience unto God by sticking with me to bring to past the vision God has given me. My three children Ai'jjon, Charles, and Kenyada I love you all so much you bring me so much joy everyday you guys make me a proud parent.

I want to thank my mother Tamara Ford, for giving birth to me and raising me and my stepfather Frank Ford for constantly having my back. My father Robert Johnson and stepmother Donna Johnson for your prayers and your love. My two brothers Al "Munch" Trotman and Joshua Ford, I am proud to have two of the most awesome brothers in the world. My grandmother Alma Carroll and my grandfather Stanley Carroll, I love you. You guys are my heart.

My favorite cousin, Ra'Shad, a.k.a Raymond, you keep me going.

To my best friend, Denzel, thank you for all your work and patience, and taking the time out to do all that you do for me.

Mrs. Marshall, my history teacher from Dupont Park Adventist, you taught me a bundle of things I carry to this day and it shows by the way I walk, talk, and carry myself and the values in which I choose to raise my family. You are also part of the reason why I am a good public speaker. You taught me that being confident and firm in what you say are the only two legs that will help you survive the fight life throws at you.

To my Creative Writing teacher, Mr. Joseph Ross, you taught me everything I know about poetry and how to establish myself poetically.

To the best Pastor in the whole world, Prophetess Buffie McIver, and Co-Pastor Bryan Wilson and the Nevi'im True Holiness Church of the Apostolic Faith, Inc, I love you guys thank you for your prayers and support.

To my aunt, Yvonne Staples, you don't know how much I appreciate you and love you. Aunt Tarsha, Latanya and cousin Brycen, I love you guys.

To my professor, Dr. Vera Jackson, thank you for allowing God to use you to lead me to that open door to birth out this book.

To the best publisher and publishing company, Pastor Irma McKnight and Kingdom Living Publishing, you have been a blessing to me and now I am going to be a blessing unto you through the grace of God we are going to make the bestseller list.

Table of Contents

Preface

"From Pain to Poetic Justice" is a book filled with poems that are inspired from pain and hurt to instill justice in a poetic sense — poetry that uplifts the down in spirit, preaches equality, and practices freedom of speech. From church to black history to current events, all make up the poems that reside in this book. Taking a stand using poetry rather than violence to express pain and anger is the method the author uses to be heard. In his work, he steps into the shoes of different people who are victims of domestic violence and who are being wrongfully judged in the church and many different areas and walks of life.

Essence of My Poetry

I manipulate my pen
to go to bed
with my paper,
to give birth
to my poetry.
The outline of my life,
drama to the extreme.

Poetry

The mediator,
between me
and the offspring of Life's first born,
reality.

Poetry

is the illustrator
who uses my tears
to poetically paint my issues
on paper.

Poetry

is my bull horn,
when I want to scream
and let the world know
my troubles.

Preface

Poetry
is a code
because you can say one thing
and somebody can read it
and to them
something else will unfold.
Leaving your deepest secrets
hidden
and still untold.

Poetry

A little here
A little there

Poetry

My language,
my replacement
of ten deep breaths
when I want to explode
in anger.

Poetry

is peace,
gives me relief,
it is my mouth piece.

CHAPTER ONE

The Church Era

Little Rock

Little Rock Baptist Church.
The little church on the corner
that makes so much noise
they make a deaf man's ears
hurt.

Oh it's a highway,
to heaven,
none can walk up there,
but the pure in heart,
walking up the king's highway.

is the hymn of the morning
that has the believer's sailing
on the boat of hope
in the sea of promises
set by the sails of faith
that God is a fountain
so refreshing
great is His mercy
and grace.

The old man
stomping his foot
showing how happy
he is that God
let him see another day.

Mother Winguard
humming to stir up

a praise she's been waiting
to release since she struck
the parking lot.

What you know bout Jesus?

He's alright!

Put yo hands together,
and put yo feet on the floor
and let the Holy Ghost
rock you from the pulpit
to the door.

If it wasn't for the Lord
who was on my side,
I don't know where
I would be.

are not just cliché's
but living testimonies
of people who just know
how to get God's attention
everyday
just by proving
that they have faith.

People clapping
as the man of God
arises and makes his way
to the podium.
The people are excited
because they know

that he carries
the Word of God in him
that he will stand
and deliver to them.
Preacher talking loud
drawing a crowd.
Sinners come in to
get their first class
ticket to heaven,
at a high price
that the blood of Jesus
has already waived,
we church folk call them
saved.

Organ starts its engine,
jumps in place
to catch up with the preacher
as he is already on a roll
as he reaches the end
of his sermon.
Bible closed
no longer reading
from his notes.
Taking deep breaths
to clears his throat.

The God that I serve, Ha!!
Is able, Ha!!
Somebody shout able!! Ha!!
He's my living water, Ha!!
My lily in the valley, Ha!!
Father, Ha!!

I stretch my hands to thee!! Ha!!
No other help I know, Ha!!
Little Rock
the feisty little church
on the corner.

A little rock

but has a better influence
than a dope dealer

A little rock

that supplies a better product
than the one sold
on the very corner on which
it resides.

A little rock

that even when
you try to toss it
in the ocean to watch
it bounce on water
and leap to its doom
in the sea of failure,
it may sink
but also does it quickly
defy gravity
and keep its head
above water
not only
disobeying the gravity law

yet proving to you
how great is their God
the writer
of the Biblical law.
A little rock

On Christ
the solid rock
I stand
all other ground
is sinking sand.

The Silent Sinner

Christians
sometimes bother me.

We are supposed to speak
the Gospel.

But we have contaminated
the tongue
and spiritual gums

with plaque
called hypocrisy.

Love one
another
as I have loved you.

Let's see if you really

are a resemblance
of these words.

You got it down

that you must not partake
alcohol as a drink.

Yet you drink
from the cup of gossip.

I remind you
that too is a sin.
You mastered it

Tithing
and the principle
that God accepts your last.

But what you never tell
is that your first
went to scratch-offs
and lottery tickets.

You understand the Scripture

Thou shall not commit
adultery,
In the physical sense.

Totally committed to Christ
so you say.
Yet,
you cheat on God
with the devil.

Allowing him
to have dominion
over your emotions.

As the head
God told you
to love your neighbor.

But because of your infected
flesh
you slander their name
with no valid reason.
But let that be you.
You'd swear up and down
they are demons
and they are just hating
on you.

You love to quote the words

Come as you are
trying to sound deep.

But let a girl
who has been out on the streets
have a desire to get it right
with Jesus.

She remembers
all she owns is a skirt
that's way above the knees.
She can hear grandma
from the past uttering,

Child come as you are
God will change your heart.

When she comes
you huddle in your clique
you mumble
Jezebel

Whoremonger
Slut
She's going to hell
cause she is fast.
But AHHHHH
how quick
do you forget
every chance you get
you try to sleep
with your pastor.

And the only reason
why you go hard
on her
is because when you see her
it's like looking in the mirror.

An image you hate
to see.

You love it when David said,

I will become more
undignified than this.

It's all gravy
until a young brother comes
in the House of God
praising His name as if he is
crazy.

You got your noise
turned upside down.

He's praising him because
he is not who he used to be.

Towards him
you make faces
because you are not pleased.
But let it be
a club beat
you're quick to prove
there is rhythm in your feet.

Nobody is better
or more saved than the other.

We are saved by grace

Not by works,
or how well you can cover up
your dirt.

For if we had it
altogether

Then tell me

what would we
need God for?

The Babe in Christ

I never thought
that a Christian man
would in my eyes
be my desire.

It's something about him,
that separates him from the rest.
He takes my hand
and helps me pray through
my problems.

He doesn't refer
to me as a bitch
or a hoe.
Nor does he just
admire me based on
how I am built
from head to toe.

Everything my boyfriend is.
He is not.
Which really amazes me
because
for a long time
I've been holding on
to this relationship.
But it seems like
a bridge to no man's land.

He's been there
to provide for me
his shoulder
in times when
I needed his Uhaul-like
shoulder to carry
my heavy load.

I look at him
different now
than the way I used to.
If he keeps it up
he may be my new boo.

He's exactly the man
every woman
displays verbally in
her "I Have a Dream Speech,"
with the girls,
on girls night out.

Just a warm embrace from him.

Just a kiss from him.

 He tenderly caresses my chin.

Just a gaze into my eyes
from him.

That is classified evidence
of how much he really loves me.

Just a whisper in my ear from him.
That are like waves of rain
that covers me
in his pool of love.

Just a lifetime with him

Woman to man,
I realized
true love lies in
the crease of his hands.

It's A God Thang

It tickles me how people try to challenge,
or logically figure out God.
They figure
because they cannot see Him,
therefore He is not there.
When the wind blows
you can't see it,
but you feel it so there must be
something there.
God is a Spirit
and those who worship Him
must worship in spirit and in truth.

You have to know that God
does not think the way we think.
His ways are not our ways.
He does not operate the way we do.
He's always two steps ahead of us.
When God promises He will work it out,
He will.

It's a God thang.

You got to believe it,
then you'll receive it.

When money is short
but somehow bills are always paid
on time

It's a God thang.

When doctors say
you don't have long to live.
But if two or three are gathered in His name
and speak life over you
and you end up living much longer

It's a God thang.

When you know people
who have been in wheelchairs
and walkers
and one Sunday morning
Pastor anoints their head
and abdomen with oil.
They get up
and start giving God stupid,
ridiculous praise

It's a God thang

When I get happy as I look back
and see how God continues
to bless me
and in spite of my faults
He sees fit to keep me
because I have favor.
But only because I recognize Him
as the Father,
I get happy
and speak in different tongues.
Don't try to understand it,
you can't logically figure it out

It's a God thang!!

The Grocery Store Experience

As I look back,
I see the traces
of my dried up tears.
Wondering,
How did I get here?

Just last year,
I had no job,
car,
along with
an impure heart.

I would come
to this same grocery store,
broke,
with my thick black coat.
strung out on drugs,
anything within arms reach
I was ready to steal.

But since,
I've been saved,
Sanctified,
Holy Ghost filled,
fire baptized.
YES,
I am healed.

As I push the shopping cart
Down aisle number seven,

I remember how I used to
Walk down this same aisle
With the devil.
He used to say,
Steal the cereal
on the shelf
for your baby girl.

Today

I walk aisle seven
with a special covering
from Heaven,
The Holy Ghost,
my shield,
and new coat.

I no longer have to hide
anything under it.
because God's glory
is all over me
for all to see.
Look at me,
an anointed exhibit.

There was a time

I could not afford
the ground beef,
because I had
no money.
To get it,
It cost me my dignity

at the expense of selling
my body in the streets.

Now

When I look back
over my life,
the Holy Spirit
overwhelms me.
My mouth begins to move
uncontrollably,
because now
I can pay for this ground beef.
Blessed by Jesus
you see.

There was a time

I would stroll down
Aisle six,
I can remember
Purposely spilling
Tomato sauce
So I could "slip,"
Hoping to get money,
So I could get me a fix.
Yelling at the manager,
I'M GOIN SUE.

BUT GOD

Has delivered me,
He deserves my praise
that's long overdue.

The Church Era

Finally

I get to aisle nine,
by now I have tears flowing
from my eyes,
my body is getting fidgety.
The utterance from my mouth
becomes loud.
God is about to use me,
through me
He's going to show up
and show out.

Ay-Shun-da-la-bosha
I say,
Aye-lah-man-see-yo,
Ah-shay-doe-doe-domosha
Toda Elohim.

You've made a way
I am more than a conqueror.

I push my shopping cart
out my way.
I take my hand
to smack the wind.
Leaping,
screaming.

All of a sudden,
God said,

I dare you to shout

A drum roll goes off
in my head.
Its purpose is to instigate,
agitate,
and introduce my praise.

Then a keyboard
goes off in my head

Dun Dun……DunDunDun
with that same pattern
repeated multiple times.

I start moving
1
2
dip
thomping,
bucking,
stomping.

Some looking
as if I had mental issues.

Others yelling,

PRAISE HIM.
WORK ON IT.
YOU BETTA MAGNIFY
THE VERY GOD OF YOUR EXISTENCE
GET IT, GET IT, GET IT

I look on the top shelf,
I see a soup of Campbell's
Chicken Noodle Soup,
and I thought of their slogan
mmm mmm good.

But taste and see
That the LORD is
mmm mmm good!!!

A Virtuous Woman

"Who can find a virtuous wife? For her worth is far above rubies. The heart of her husband safely trusts her; so he will have no lack of gain. She does him good not evil all the days of her life" (Proverbs 31:10-12).

In today's society
it is hard to find a woman
just right for me.
Females today
can be so trifling.
Some just give up
their bodies
oh so easily.

It don't take much
to get between their legs,
to enjoy all the pleasures
of "Happy Hour."
Some of them,
all you gotta do
is dot every "I"
and cross
every "T."
Say all the right things
to connect the dots
and Bingo
Yahtzee
Monopoly
Jinga

WE HAVE ADMISSION.
Where is the woman
Momma always talks about?

Where is the woman

Who will make you chase her
just to see what you really want
from her?
And when you will go the distance
she will know it is her essence
that you long for?

Where is the woman

Who is loyal
and because
of her honesty
it is the reason why
it's her you spoil?

Where is the woman

Who is excited
about making it to church
every Sunday?
And don't mind clinging
to your hand while stomping
on the devil's head
when you give God praise?

Where is the woman

Who has the body of Beyonce
Independence of Oprah
and intelligence of Michelle Obama?
Where is the woman

Who keeps you grounded
when you start to sink?
Who lets you know if
you're too far out there
and will let you know
if your attitude stinks?

Where is the woman

Who will let a man
be a man?
Who will allow a man's
arms to be her chariot
as he navigates the way
to the bedroom
to make passionate love to her?

Where is the woman?

Who can discern the difference
between a no good man
and the one she's been looking for?
One who can look at a man on site,
and already know he
ain't worth two cents.

Where is the woman?

Well,
A virtuous woman
is like a ruby,
she's rare,
and hard to find.
I guess I can't find her
because God
is preparing her for me.
The perfect match.

A virtuous man
and a virtuous woman,
a perfect image of what
a relationship is supposed
to look like.

A relationship
with a halo over it
that lets you know,
God has His hands all over it.

A virtuous woman

my dream girl
who makes me happy.

A virtuous woman

Who will help me
get through rough nights.

A virtuous woman

Not just any woman.

The Preacher

I am the "Man of God."
Some know me as
the preacher
who always talks about
prosperity.
Check my record,
I've never given a dime
to charity.

I have 10 bodyguards,
whom I pay a hell of
a good salary.
Armorbearers,
who guard me
like a celebrity.

See, I pastor thousands
in a mega church.
I made love
to sister Loretta
in my office
behind my desk.

Then that fine new member
Monique
in the audio booth.

Oh, and I can't forget
the deacon's wife
Simone.

Me and her in the pulpit,
as I had her posted up
on the podium as if I frisked
her for illegal drugs.

I regret that day
because it was the day me
and Simone created
my illegitimate child,
who looks like me,
talks like me,
but on his birth certificate
it says Deacon William Black
as the sower of my seed.

I live the life of a millionaire.
Bentley
to a Rolls Royce.
Armani suits,
which I never wear the same suit
twice.
But yet I wipe the dust off
of them every Sunday,
as I open the doors of the church
and tell the lost
to come to Christ.

Only to manipulate them.
And because
of my millionaire status,
I make it hard for them
to get in touch with me,
their pastor

if they are going through
a dilemma.
But it all comes to an end.
When one Sunday I stand
in the presence of
the most high God.
Misinterpreting Scripture
to justify my own sinful living.
The day my chariot
swings low
and catches up to me.

When a guy in plain view
walked down
center isle towards my pulpit.
Stops me in the middle of my sermon.
He yells,

This is for sleeping with my wife
and fathering the only child
I've been taking care of for three years.

He shoots me
in the core of my chest.
Because of the upbeat tempo
of my heart
and the rush of adrenaline
I go into cardiac arrest.
And here I am
dead in front of
my congregation
in my heaven
my abode.

With the force of passion
my killer thrust his bullet
of vengeance
into my temple.
I say my last words.

Ashes to ashes
dust to dust,
because of my uncrucified flesh
my body shall turn to rust.

The Preacher Boy

When people see me
they recognize me as
a child of God.
You would think my life is
easy but in reality it's
hard.

Sunday after Sunday,
I preach from my belly,
speaking with authority,
making demons go ballistic.
With the mic in my right hand
and my hand towel in the other.
I shout to my congregation,
*"Look at your neighbor and say
I love you like a brother."*

On the outside,
I appear strong and uplifted in spirit,
but on the inside I hurt
and deep down I question.

Why is it most females
claim they want a good man,
but choose the very opposite?
A man with a subpoena in one hand
and a paper that says his urine
is dirtier then the Anacostia River
in the other?

They claim they want a gentle-man,
but he never strokes you
with the swift velocity of his love
by sweeping you off your feet.

They claim they want somebody,
who is going to bring something
to the table. But he refuses to work
because he's not used to hard labor.

Why is it that men like me
are always overlooked?
You asked God for a good man,
but you don't recognize me
when you see me.
Or welcome me with open arms.

You call for me, send a word
out to the head man upstairs
every night in your prayers,
but you never receive me.

Why do you take my kindness
for weakness?
Because I encourage you
rather than tear you down.
You take my kindness for
weakness.

Because I'd rather hold you at night,
than have fist fights.
Why do you take my kindness
for weakness?

Maybe if I blacken your eyes
just a little bit and shower you
with words that singe you,
along with the saliva that stains you.
Maybe you will recognize me.

If I help you lower your self-esteem just
a little bit, you'll recognize me and
claim with assurance that behind
every blow, I truly love you.

If I prohibit you from seeing your
family, you'll think it's cute
because I want to keep you to
myself. Maybe you'll recognize me
then.

If I no longer respect you,
refer to you as my bottom hoe.
Only good for one thing,
can't even remember your last name
but got you in my phone as "Bust it Baby."
You'll recognize me then, won't you?

So stop asking the same question,
"Where are the good men?"
Half of the time you look them in the
face every day.

But because he refused to let the ghetto come
out of him, you saw it as him
being weak and lacking in his
masculinity pushing him away.
Don't take my kindness for weakness.

The True Meaning of Fornication

Sex
outside of marriage.
It's not just the physical.
It is also spiritual.

Some preachers,
commit adultery
on their first love,
God.

To fornicate
with the devil,
to produce a seed
of deadly fate.

Using the pulpit
to manipulate,
to control,
to promote themselves
to a celebrity status.
And their sermons,
are no longer
about Jesus.

Taking advantage
of kind-hearted folk.
Deteriorating the once preserved office
of a pastor.
Treating the office
of a pastor as a game.

So they run a train
on the people of God,
by bringing like-minded preachers
to their pulpit.
Forever sugarcoating
their love,
fascination
and lust for money
with the "prosperity gospel" preaching.

Becoming petty,
excommunicating themselves
from their congregation.

Dipped in this ministry
like a strawberry in chocolate.
Your eagerness
to get to know God
is whipped out by
their "doctrine."

Eliminating Christ
out of the equation.
Now you tell me,
what or who
really nowadays
commits the biggest sin?

CHAPTER TWO

The Romantic Era

Holy Ghost Girl

Holy Ghost Girl

An observation
of a REAL WOMAN
also known as a
Virtuous Woman,
has beauty that passes
the final exam
of the outside appearance,
we know that as
the only depths in which
a fool would go
in search for a wife
which is only a short distance.

What makes her different from the rest?
Something about her caught me
considering her as a new contestant.

She is what we
Men of God
know as

A Holy Ghost Girl

Virtuous
nothing about her is mysterious
because she's upfront.
What she does behind closed doors
is not dangerous,

toward us,
because she reads the Word
and stays prayed up.

A Holy Ghost Girl

she's 20 something years of age
hmm
and she's a nice chapter
in the book of Excellent Qualities
of a Wife,
but because I'm only 17,
To many I am too young,
I might as well turn
the page.

A Holy Ghost Girl

Though she is gorgeous
on the outside.
When we embrace
it isn't the curves
of the waist
that first come to mind,
because she is so far
beyond that.

With an Associate's Degree
in common sense,
a Bachelor's
in a Perfect Example of
a Woman,
Christian.

A Master's Degree in
conquering a rough society
while holding a PhD
in Praiseology.

A Holy Ghost Girl

Not just a piece
that a man only invites
on a first class trip
to his bed.
But a gift from God
who keeps a man rooted
in the garden of righteousness
when demons start messing
with his head.

A Holy Ghost Girl

Our hugs
meaning that we touch
and agree,
we are pleased to see
each other,
my first thought
is not sexual
but impressed,
because of her intellectual,
yet scary because if she
has all I want then
why is it so difficult
to take my chances
and pursue her,

building a bond
so successful.

A Holy Ghost Girl

So when I began
to doubt my faith
she'll guide me back
saying
God is still everything
while caressing the hairs
on my chin
gazing me in the face.

A Holy Ghost Girl

Definitely what God
referred to in the good book
of Proverbs,
and when I touch her hand,
I see my future,
the smile of angels well pleased,
and happiness
licensed by God
in the crease of
her palms,
as she ventures in my eyes
realizing I am her
Psalm 27:23.

Ventilation of a Broken Heart

How did I go
from enjoying
being the target
of Cupid's rage,
to depression
buying my heart
at a price anxiety
gladly waived.

Being in love with someone,
is supposed to be
a beautiful experience
but why did it end
with me becoming acquainted
with the nagging
temper tantrum of my feelings?

I hurt

because you were about to leave
and you weren't even going to stop
and say
good bye.

I hurt

because you had me going
like time
never stopping,
at each second it was

I LOVE YOU.
Until you decided
to let go.
I'll never forget
when I heard
those words
that tampered with my skin
clinging like a magnet
scorching my skin
leaving a bruise
only to just say
I'm sorry
which was really like
salt on a wound.

I hurt

maybe because I opened up
to you too soon,
listen to what you are saying,
you said you loved me
was it ever true?
Now it's amnesia
you speak to me now
as someone you never knew
Or is this what you call
"The New You."

How do I face you
and be at peace?
There is bitterness
and hatred that wants to
reside in me.

But I got to forgive
or else I'll never be
at ease.
Why did I allow myself
to hold this paper
as my tears leap
on this clean sheet
and become the writer
of this motion picture,
Poetry.

Thankful
that there is a God
who gives strength
to face tough times
you want to resist,
though it was a joy
to experience
what I thought was
eternal bliss.
Yes it will be greatly missed.

But it's good to know
when you are faithful
God keeps on blessing.
That I take this experience
as a lesson
and it was my faith
that God was testing,
to see
that when people leave
will I lean on God
almighty?

This too shall pass
baby girl I admit
it was a blast,
for I still have my joy
no more contrite spirit
I am at peace
at last.

A Dozen Roses -The Love Affair

Flowers are the correct path of what love is suppose to be.
They don't boast about how pretty they are, or how perfect
they are for you to possess. They just simply show you with
their essence, which is their beauty.

A dozen roses
just for you.
A dozen roses
each one with a meaning
inspired by you.

A red rose
means I love you
like how a toddler loves Barney,
how a bee loves honey,
and how Bugs adored Lola Bunny.

A coral rose
for you
a symbol of my passion,
desire to be with you,
life everlasting.

A lavender rose
is evidence
of how I fell in love
with you at first sight.

An orange rose
because I'm fascinated
by your simplicity
urging me to desire
your intimacy.

A peach rose
because I appreciate
the friendship
which is the energy
that ignites my attention
when you sway past
my radar.

A pink rose
because lately
you've graced
my dreams
with your smile
that can calm a sizzled nerve.

A white rose
because I realized
the truth,
that I'm so into you.

A yellow rose
for the joy
you brought me
over the last few months
the highlights of my day
when we spent time together at lunch.

A blue rose
because you're a mysterious
work of art
and I want to find the right words
to the puzzle
so I can win the key
to your heart.

A turquoise rose
because I can
look in your eyes
and constantly find peace
no more do I want you to tease
but to trust me
as we enjoy the fruits
of love when it's released.

A gold rose
because I simply
care about you.
The joy I would get
if for five minutes
I could just hold you.

Finally,
a black rose
for me
if you ever left me
for eternity
a piece
or even a trace of you
would still be with me.

A dozen roses
just for you.
A dozen roses
each one with a meaning
inspired by you.

Love's Sacrifices

Love
causes a person
to make sacrifices.
It can cause you
to make yourself uncomfortable
so he or she can reside
in the comfort of the bliss
that you shower them with.

I will do anything for love

gracefully place my jacket
over your shoulders as we walk
in nippy weather, as I whisper
intimacy's love ballad
in your ear.

I will do anything for love

Open the door to let you in first
which is what we know
as chivalry.
With my actions I show you
that I am dehydrated
and in need of your love
let me dig from your well
for my happiness is thirsty.

I will do anything for love

Come and sweep you off your feet
leaving a dust trail that
spells out
Stamped, she's mine.

But I will not

let you think that because I
am a child of God that it gives
you lead way to walk over me,
thinking I won't put you in your place
and let your selfishness
disfigure the happiness on my face.

You will not

take my kindness as a weakness
thinking you've got the best
of me
'cause trust and believe you'll pay
'cause I serve a God who has appointed
His men to put a hedge of protection
over me.
You screw over His own,
and you'll screw over your own destiny.

I will not

play the fool
and let you think you've got me
wrapped around your finger
and putting me in the pocket,
please
this is not a game of pool.

You will

respect me

You will

realize that I'm not one
to be played with,
and if you think I'm playing
must I add
that I serve a God who
constantly turns unbelievers
into believers
must I do the same?
All I need you to do
is give me a reason to.

I will do anything for love

But I will not

let you degrade
and disrespect me
in any way
because I can do that
all
by
my
self

Summer Love

As of this moment,
I tried to find
an excellent entrée
to be served in this here
poem
as my subject.
Only one image
came to mind
and her face
I dare not reject.

It's so easy
to use the same old line
There's something different
about her.
Or just lust over her
based on the architecture,
or mental pleasure
she provides
with just one look
at her backside.

But

She does write my poetry
because she is the ink
from the well
known as the pen
that stains the paper

causing me to blow the words
and watch them scatter.

Why don't I want
this poem
to high-five the genre
of *Love Poems*?
Because I am
not
in love with her,
besides
it would only be me
just thinking that I am
a guy she'd prefer.

When she talks
there's a letter that evaporates
off of her tongue sounding
like an *S*
because Summer Love
is her foreign language
something I wish
I had.

When she lectures
from her only reference
her heart,
about Romantic Love
between a man
and a woman
it's hard to not notice
that she tells the truth
having myself to pinch myself

reminding myself,
Man she's not even talking
about you.

The idea would be
to fall for someone
who knew how to get
through the maze
in your heart,
retrieve the key,
only to leave you signing
your name on a degree
that says they're certified
in knowing how to make you
happy.

Why was it so hard for me
to write a poem contaminated
with lusty words to describe
the blue print of her chest
than to write this here poem
stamped with sincerity
at its best?

Maybe because a week
from now,
my reminiscence of you
now translated
into these words
will shatter
like glass
only to be neglected
becoming evidence

of a happy thought
of you
not handled with care.

Summer Love
is nothing but realness
composing a harmony
of prolific words
molded into my poetry.

Blue Moon

Walking as my heart
is weighed down
by sorrow
and depression.
Life has taken more
from me than the economy has
in this recession.

I came to this beach
in the midst of darkness
where not a soul can bear witness
to the agony and grief in my eyes.
They wonder where
this body of water came from.
Filled with my tears
which I've shed
throughout the years.

My deepest secrets
are gathered together
under this blue moon,
surrounded by stars
that represent each day
that has been a living hell for me.

From my fears to my desires,
from good moments,
to walking through hell's fire
my life is as rough as
the sand of the beach.

Happiness
and peace
just seem so far
out of my reach.

CHAPTER THREE

Society

Brother Man

Brother man
Brother man
what is the matter
with you?
What have you become?
No responsibility
do you take
for your mistakes.
Instead you play victim.

Brother man
Brother man

Why do you
continue to
fulfill society's prophecy
that you are
more likely to
be a citizen
of a penitentiary
than to graduate
at 21 earning
your first Bachelor's Degree.

Brother Man
Brother Man

Please,
tell me
where is the joy

in loving
to have fatigue
because you
run the streets,
playing *peek-a-boo*
with the police.

Brother Man
Brother Man

Why is it so,
that the only time
you decide to speak
your mind
is when you throw up gang signs?

Where are you
and your "*mans
and them*" collective voices
when the system slaps you
in the face
With blows of *A.D.H.D,*
throwing you in a classroom
because they want to make a point
that you're slow
and you can't read.
But you come together
over a bag of weed.

Brother Man
Brother Man

Why is
living in the moment
your only vision
in site
at this point in time
in your life?
Maximize the meaning of your life,
and rewrite what a black man
is supposed to look like.

Brother Man
Brother Man

There is so much
about this life
you have to grasp
and understand.
there is more
to life that you
need to learn
far beyond your neighborhood.
Knowledge,
you need to have understood.

Brother Man
Brother Man

Excellent education,
meeting all self-expectations,
obtaining all fruits of the spirit
as talked about
in the book of Galatians

are not elements of life
our ancestors would want you to
refuse.

But you do,
by making
a premature decision
causing the birth
of your purpose
to go wrong.

By your mishandling
of the destiny
the Almighty
has placed in your belly
you cause your own
miscarriage.
assassinating your dream
at the womb.

Brother Man
Brother Man

All you're worried about
is how you look
in *Black Label*
rather than
dressing yourself
in the Holy Ghost,
in His blood
a substance
that can save you.

Brother Man
Brother Man

Put your flesh
to sleep
let your life
be the ink
to interfere with the flow
of history.

Lastly,
don't just live life
being a *"Brother Man"*
you have options man.

You can be

Mr. Man,
Her man,
God's chosen man,
The man,
With a master plan
A Dr.
with a plan.

That baby's daddy
who took care of his kid
like a man.

A man who lived
like a man.

And a man
who died as a man.

Not another Statistic

All these stereotypes
about black men
are getting on my nerves.
Behind our backs
they call us names
which are so absurd.

They call us

gangsters
hoodlums
and sometimes go as far as
to referring to us as
you people.
I thought the Constitution said,
We The People.

Because I walk down the street
with a North Face coat on
with my hands in my pocket
you cling to your purse
as if at any moment
I'll clean you out at gun point.

Because of the way I wear my hair
or even dap my friends on the street
you think I belong to a gang.

No
I am not another statistic.
Why are my people looked at
differently?

If you are white
and gun enthusiastic
you are patriotic.

But if you are black
and you carry a gun
that makes you a thug.

Something is wrong with that picture.
For too long
we have been oppressed.
well now we will stand up
and show the world our best
nothing less
and that we will never let it rest.

Walk Don't Run

Life is short,
Live it slowly
not fast like a
Southwest airline
departing from a
airport.

Everyday counts,
because you should
leave a legacy
with an impact
of an enormous
amount.

It is important in
life to
walk and not run.

As a toddler when you
grace the earth with
your footsteps

Walk don't run

When you make your way
to the prom and you want
everybody to see how smooth
your swagger is

Walk don't run

When they call your name
at graduation.
Take 12 steps for 12 years
of homework
detention
late nights
and those times
when you almost faced suspension.
Make sure you

Walk don't run.

When you walk through
the valley and the shadow
of death and you feel like
no one understands you and
you feel the world is against you.

Walk don't run

When they hauled
Rosa Parks off to
the jailhouse
for going toe to toe
with injustice

She didn't run she walked.

When Jesus went from
the garden of Gethsemane
to the six hours of carrying
heavy burdens to the hills
of Calvary.
He didn't run He walked

When Martin Luther King Jr.,
from 1929-1968,
went from Atlanta, Georgia,
to a life time trip around the world
spreading the Gospel
all the way to Memphis, Tennessee,
to have a meeting with death
on a hotel balcony

He didn't run he walked

When brother Malcolm X
went to Mecca and saw
a diverse group of people
together for one cause
only to come back to America
and try to correct what had been
wrongly taught,
only to result in a
first class trip to an early grave.

He didn't run from it but he walked.

When you find yourself
Against the wall and it seems
Like you can't escape,
Show your strength
Just keep on going and

Walk don't run.

CHAPTER FOUR

Domestic Violence

A Mighty Blow

With his fist

he slams on the podium
every Sunday as he preaches
parallel to the sound of the organ.

With his fist

he covers the cage in which lies
his endangered species,
his tongue,
filled with power
of the living God,
yet contaminated,
with insults,
and the breath
of a violent demon.

With that same fist

He thrust into my mouth
to mute all sound
as he engulfs my body
like a lion on a zebra.

With that same fist

He recoils my head
against the wall,
With that same fist

He used my temple
to sharpen the boundaries
of his knuckles.

But with my fist

I strike back
with rage
and a mindset
that enough
was enough.

With my fist

I plunged back
the fist of a now
crazy
deranged
filled with aggression
mad battered woman.

With my fist

I let go
bit by bit
dirt
over his dead carcass.

The S.R.A.G.E of a Woman

With his Strength

He overpowered me,
for the short period
of time he resided
is his pleasure
on top of me,
thrusting himself in me.
He used his moans
to sugarcoat this here wrong.

With his Rage

Fueled with his insecurity
he drove down a path
in my life
called purity
That was set as off limits
for the Man of God
designed for me.

With his Apathy

His no show of emotions
dared to caress my fear,
me in anger
I dared not to prolong my tears.

With his Gender

He thought he automatically
was dominant
over me.

With his Endurance

He cared less about my pain
my respect he once had,
my image
and my review of him is no longer
the same.

But with my Strength

Not only did I have the ability
to prevail the ordeal,
but I forgave him,
still I am strong
the value of my self-esteem
he could not steal.

With my Rage

Fueled with stability
I put my rage on the road
running over his defeat
over me.

With my Apathy

I put aside my feelings
to kill my offender.
Instead I leaned on GOD

because I AM HIS,
my dilemma
automatically became a priority
on His agenda.

With my Gender

It was no longer a debate
on who was dominant
male
or female
only the strong survive
never having to degrade
the other to stamp
with assurance that He is
a male

With my Endurance

I now understand why
victory is not given to the swift
and the strong,
but to the ones who endure
until the end
because in one point in time
they knew what it felt like
to be trampled over
by the iron feet of their oppression,
and they understand that bad days,
sleepless nights
are only phases in life
that only last for a semester.
So that is their notion

to keep pushing until
they can look the ones
who hurt them in the eye
and forgive them
real easy on the first try
because they are now
at the state of peace
where they
now reside.

Strength

Rage

Apathy

Gender

Endurance

THE S.R.A.G.E of A WOMAN

CHAPTER FIVE

Black History

306 Lorraine Motel

As I step foot onto this balcony,
I greet everyone standing beside and below me.
Last night
I gave a speech that was a part of my cleansing,
but little did I know,
within the next few moments,
I would enter another dimension.

"It's kind of cold out Doc, you should go back in
and grab an overcoat."
 I tilt my head up to feel a breeze,
 unlike no other.
It felt like the breath of death, coming to claim my temple.

Before I could even step back into my "King-Abernathy"
suite, a bullet pierces my jaw, travels down through
my spinal cord, knocking me off of my feet.
I lay tranquilized on the ground,
as my blood becomes acquainted with the rusty
concrete on the balcony.

I look over to my right,
and I see my good friend,
Rev. Ralph Abernathy.
He puts a towel over my face
to stop the blood from flowing.
"Martin, it's Ralph. Everything
is going to be okay." But,
I realized April 4, 1968,
would be my transition day.

As I lay on my rugged,
soiled,
death bed
that is contaminated,
with the footsteps of rats and roaches,
I see a quick slideshow of the life I live.

From the precious moments with "Yoki,"
Bernice,
Dexter,
and "Marti"
To the sentimental moments
with Coretta.

My living is not in vain

From Montgomery to Memphis,
From "The Drum Major" to "I Have a Dream,"
From the Ku Klux Klan, to SCLC,

My living is not in vain.

From John F. Kennedy to Medgar Evers.
No greater love,
than one who will lay down his life for
a friend.
No.

My living is not in vain.

I soak every last moment of life
with pride.
Even though I can't respond when they call my name.

My voice,
taken by the impact
of hatred,
jealousy,
and envy,
all in one vicious bullet.
I strain and mumble the shattered words
of my favorite melody,

"Precious Lord,
take my hand. Lead me on, let me stand
I am tired, I am weak, I am worn
Through the storm, through the night
Lead me on to the light
Take my hand precious Lord, lead me home."

I end this phase of life,
slipped away, into the bosom
of Jesus Christ.

As my devoured physical shell remains,
others hope it will be saved from an already
declared unconscious sleep.
My Blood
leaves a smeared writing on the concrete that says,
"Martin Luther King, Jr. was here, 1929-1968.
Rest in peace."

On November 4, 2008

On November 4, 2008
a shift in America took place.
Citizens of this great nation,
both young and old.
Whites
blacks,
Native Americans
and Latinos

went out to exercise
their right to vote.

I stayed home
to watch God show up
and show out
and let the world know
that it was Obama's time
to blossom and sprout.

Just to think we started out
as slaves.
Brought over on ships
like the Amistad.
Confused
abused
not knowing
what the road was like ahead.

Being lynched
because we spoke up
saying,
We'd rather die on our feet
than keep living on our knees.

Always being told
we were three fourths
of a human being
therefore we weren't
even included in the nation
when the Constitution was created.

We went from slavery to Malcolm X
and Martin Luther King
who dreamed that one day
we would be equal.
Fighting back with nonviolence
which did resist
and because he had faith
God was in the midst.

Sacrificing their lives
so we can live the lives we live.
Just when we thought
it would never happen
God blessed us with a man
who prevailed against all odds.
Serving a God whom he knew
could do anything but fail.

Even though
we were always told
we were last
and a minority,
He proved that eventually
the first will be last
and the last shall be first.

As I sat there
and witnessed the news say

*Barack Obama
is the new president.*

tears began to well up in my eyes
and all I could think about
was the song we sing in church.

*We've come this far
by faith.*

*Leaning on the Lord
trusting in His Holy Word
He never failed me yet.*

I can see the vision
of Dr. King in heaven
as he lifts up his hands
praising God filled with joy.

Black History

I saw Obama's grandmother
looking down saying,

That's my boy.

So you see
we are more than conquerors.
Obama proved we can
do anything
and as an African American
he showed he wasn't just
another statistic.

I'm the head
and not the tail,

I'm above
and never beneath.

I'm blessed.

But most of all
I'm proud to be
an African American.

A Harlem Night

It's about that time
on this Harlem night.
Where every cool cat drapes
on the corner of 33rd and G street.
after the street lights.

Men of all colors
young and old, waiting
to see "Cool Breeze"
put this show on a roll
As I lace up my shoes

I can feel my heart beat,
like a crescendo.
The guys chanting,
"*GO, GO, GO.*"
I step out,
shuffling from my heel
to my toes.

BING BANG, SPLIT
TATANG. SPIT CHIT
RAH BIT BIT BIT!!!
As I move and slide
against the concrete.

My feet go into auto pilot,
as I move to the rhythm
of the Harlem streets.
Sirens,

garbage,
winos
and last weeks trash
all around me.

Now that's what I call life
and it sounds sweet.
As people look from their windows,
store fronts,
and car windows.
They see the way I move

and become mesmerized
some say I float on air.
Others say I'm light on my feet.
Minority say he's a little weak,
majority say he's too good
to dance on the streets.

Well
I say,
I'm just dancing
to the beat of the Harlem streets.

Club 31 in 1931

1931 in Harlem, New York,
Club 31 is where all the big times come,
to relax, perform, or have a drink of some sort.
Anything can happen in this room.
The smell of whiskey, chicken wings,
and all sorts or perfume.
Men dressed to impress
with their custom made tuxedos,
hair slicked back,
perfect crease in their pants
looking together and in tact.
Women with their fine dresses
some with a split going up on the side.
Men gawking because they are pleasing unto
the eyes.

Lights dim as everyone is moved
and hypnotized as they watch
Lena Horne sing, "Stormy Weather."
While Cab Calloway smoothly slides
and glides across the stage, singing "Minnie the Moocher."
"Bartender get one for the lady."
"Excuse me miss, may I have this dance?"
People moving,
grooving,
women swaying their hips,
as men hold them while they dip
with a tight grip.

"Encore, encore we want more."
As Mr. Bojangles steals the show
tapping to the beat of a different drummer.
Sssssip Pa ti, Sssssip Pa ti, Sssssip Pa ti
Plack,
Pa teet, pa taht, Bah do Bop, Bah do dat
Burrrrr da boom , burrrr da boom,
doom doom doom doom doom doom doom Hey.

Everyone singin,
dancing, enjoying themselves.
The room is filled with velocity
as the Nicholas Brothers defy
gravity tapping with feeling,
doing splits,
moving their bodies like twizzlers.
Little Harold Nicholas, singing
with a smile *"Lucky Number, I'm
dreaming of Lucky Number"*   He
shouts go ahead Fayard. As he
does dance moves that were
not even invented yet, like the Mashed Potatoes,
camel walk, doing back flips,
spins,
splits,
and summersaults.

In this place you see it all.
People gathered in one room
to squeeze the sweet juice of
 "the good times" out of life's
rough lemons.

The room filled with the stench
of lust and love as Langston Hughes
gives the benediction of the night.

"The night is beautiful,
so the faces of my people.

The stars are beautiful.
So the eyes of my people.

Beautiful, also, is the sun.
Beautiful, also, are the souls of my people."

CHAPTER SIX

"Christmas Tales"

"The Homeless Man"

7:30 at night and a week before Christmas.
I push my cart with the little bit I own
down the Boulevard at the Capital Centre in Largo.
Smiling, acting normal as I am serenaded by
James Brown over the loud speakers, *"Santa Claus
Go straight to the ghetto."*

I stop in front of "Harold Pener Men of Fashion."
Looking through the frosted window watching men
try on tailored made suits. Cut right, looking tight, and
fitting nice. I began to think about how once upon
a time that was me buying expensive gifts. But for
the past 10 years my life has taken a change in shifts.

*"Excuse me young man, do you have any change
you can spare me?"* As I asked what looked like a
16 year-old as he was texting on his sidekick. He
Replied, "Naw man, go somewhere and get a job
stop being lazy." Little did he know how I became
homeless. I lost my job, my house, my only child to
leukemia and my wife to my first cousin.

Hours passed and I decided to lay my head on the
bench outside of Harold Pener, in the freezing cold.
I watched my carbon-dioxide float through the air.
I thought to myself how did I come from a luxurious
5 bedroom house to sleeping in park benches
sharing bunks with alley cats and a dirty mouse.

I drifted off into a cold sleep, with tears welling up
in my eyes. It's so cold they're turning into icicles.
I woke up the next morning amazed. In my hand
was 200 dollars in an envelope with a note. "Dear
Raymond, take this 200 dollars as a gift. I have arranged
for you to get fitted for a nice suit, at Harold Pener

so you can look presentable for a job interview I
have lined up for you, that I am guaranteed you'll get.
Don't worry about paying for the suit, tell them
"anonymous" sent you and they'll tell you
everything you need to know Merry Christmas,
much love anonymous."

"The Rich Boy"

Man I can't wait until Christmas. I got
Like 34 things on my list. I want that new
Ipod nano. Pops said he was going give me
$1,000 to go shopping. Man I cannot wait.
Walking through this outlet scoping out
What I want for Christmas.

So much to choose from, so much to look
Forward to. *"Excuse me young man, do you*
Have any change you can spare me?" A
Homeless man asked me as I whipped out
My sidekick. I said *"Naw man, go some*
Where and get a job; stop being lazy."

What is wrong with people nowadays?
Don't want to work, forget the poor. I
Don't even give them crumbs from my tray.
As long as I got what I wanted that's all
That matters to me. I can just imagine how
Many gifts are going under the tree.

I get home and I am shocked at what I saw.
People were moving everything on our front
Lawn. My dad, was nowhere to be found, still
Confused why all of our expensive belongings
Are on the dirty ground. I asked the man. *"Excuse*
Me but why are you on our private property."
He said, *"Look kid I got a job to do. The mortgage company is*
Putting you out, because the mortgage is five
Months over due."

"The Business Man"

Boy oh boy, Christmas time is a fun time.
People come in and out my store, buying gifts.
Men getting suits, high priced shoes. People ready
To buy and some have not a clue. Money, money,
Money, cha-ching, cha-ching. Everytime I see
Money, I get an ecstatic feeling.

I remember a time I didn't have too much of nothing.
Every Christmas I always give back. Because
I remember once upon a time there was a
Period where I lacked. This one homeless man
I always see stands outside my shop but never
Comes in.

He always sleeps outside on the same bench.
This Christmas I thought I should sow into his
Life. When the store closed he was asleep as I
Expected, bundled up on this little old bench.
I decided to hook him up this Christmas. I put
$200 in his hand in an envelope, promising him
A new suit and job. Now that's what Christmas is
All about, giving back, because once there was someone
Who gave back to you.

CHAPTER SEVEN

Family Matters

A Life Medley

Me and my son
sitting in his room
bonding
to a beautiful tune.

It's a tune

The crescendo
of his laughter
when I teach him
how to write a poem
which is his father's craft.

It's a tune

showing him
that like notes on a scale
life will take you
up and down.
But it's how you edit your mistakes
that will help you excel.

It's a tune

like a bridge
in a James Brown medley.
Behind the scenes
I am training him
to be a man

in areas where society
tries to mislead.

It's a tune

like a person
in their car
adjusting the bass
and treble buttons
to get the right sound.
Adjusting his wrongs
when he falls
to pick himself off the ground.

It's a tune

like an echo
the sweet sound
of his legacy
still hanging around
even when he's buried
in the ground,

like a spirit
it is lost
not to be found.

But like the wind
because of its touching breeze
you know somewhere it's still around.

Thank You (A Poem for my Mother)

For 20 years you've been
the one lady who always
bossed me around,
my number one fan
as a toddler when I
acted like a clown.

When I had eczema
you didn't rub my skin
with ointment,
instead you used to
sooth me with
comfort.

And when I had asthma attacks
with just one touch you declared
that in the name of Jesus
the devil had to take his tight grip
off of my lungs.

You couldn't teach me how
to be a man.
But you taught me
how to treat a woman

It was you who taught me
at an early age that everything
I called "mine"
came from God.

It was you

who willingly promoted yourself
as the tissue that wiped away
sorrow's waterfalls from my eyes.

It was you

who when I had low self-esteem
you never hesitated to utter to me
I was the most beautiful thing
roaming the earth.

It was you

who took on the roll of a father
and was ready to bump heads
with anyone who tried to take
advantage of me.

But what you will forever be

is my mother.
I am lucky because
I have all in one.

A mother
a father,
provider
comforter
a praiser
and a perfect example
of what a woman should be.
I would not make it this far

Family Matters

if I didn't have you to push me
and sacrifice to make sure I see
May 21st,
My graduation day.

Parents are not perfect,
but they do the best they can.
You may think they don't understand
but they do.
Just remember when you cry
they cry too.

When you smile
they smile right
back at you.

Up until now our parents
have taken care of us.
Now it is time for us
to do our part
and take care of them
by doing them one favor

on May 21st walk across the stage
with dignity
values
and giving them hope
that one day their words
of encouragement and
moral values
will not be in vain
but will be manifested
as you represent them
in life.

A Father's Love

How long must I suffer?
How much of my blood
has to be shed?
It is bad enough they stuck
more then twenty holes
in my head.

I look like a fool
letting this world tear me
limb from limb.
But these are things
only a father will do
for his children.

It seems as if
it is all happening
in slow motion.
They punctured holes
the size of oranges
into my flesh,

my blood gushing out
as I lay helpless.
I screamed,
I cried,
but I never complained.

Instead I remained silent
and stretched high

before the world,
as my wounds poured
out my blood and my sweat.

By now
I know what has to happen next.
But at the same time I feel
perplexed.

After a while my body
became numb
and I could no longer
raise my body up
to take a breath.

They spit on me
and questioned
my authority
and dared me
to spare my life.

But I had to take responsibility
for my children's actions.
So I stayed there
and just threw my head back.

Then I said my final words,
all of a sudden my body started
to feel cold and began to freeze.
Then I began to get sleepy,
my eyes got heavy
as if a ton of weights
were pulling them down.

I dropped my head
in the locks of my shoulders
I gave up the yokes,
and I expired.

Blood of My Father

Daddy daddy,
you are the best.
You taught us how to be a family.
This picture says a thousand words
about your legacy.
You prospered in the time of recession.
Through depression you challenged it
with ruthless aggression.

While other black families taught
their children to fear
the white man.
You instilled in us to show equality,
and to strike back love,
with an open hand.

You faced hatred with the smile
of patience,
because you knew society
was built to count you out.
Only because they feared
not
your thoughts
but your abilities.

While they strike you with
shotguns,
nooses,
and clinched fists.

You retaliated
with your leg crossed
and worked your way
up to the point where
you signed off their paychecks.

You made it possible for them
to buy the abundant supply of nooses
they once
threatened your life with.

You made society have no option,
but to lay out the carpet you non-selfishly
shared and graced your footsteps with,
even those who willingly and without
hesitation had an all expense paid,
planned,
trip to your early resting place.

Above all you were my daddy.
Through me you live because it is
your blood that sustains every aspect of
my history.

It was the blood of my father
they yearned for,
because it was rich
valuable
intimidating
a threat
and prosperous.

It was his blood
he left on the wall
when they took his life.

*"No man takes my life,
I lay it down."*

The blood in me,

blood of my history

blood of my ancestors

blood,

of my father.

About Me

In the Name of......

As I sit at the window
in this office building
looking over in the inner streets
of Southeast D.C.
I can feel the spirit
of my future roaming
a few opened doors
ahead of me.

The street is 1800 Martin Luther King
when I realized
also
is my name great
very soon will there be
a street named after me.

It is amazing to know
that greats such as
Langston Hughes
have walked these streets.

While Frederick Douglass stayed
not far from the house
where I sleep.

Johnny Gill
tuning up his vocals
every Sunday
in the church
giving God a thrill.

And Chuck Brown
creating his own genre
of music.
The only artist
with a five letter first name
and last name,
Brown
who wasn't James Brown
but with his tunes you could get down.
Whose hit wasn't

I know you got soul

but

Run Joe!!
With the police
knockin at the doe.

Washington, D.C.,
the real "Graceland"
because many icons
have come out of
this diamond city.

Many names
who when mentioned
would ring Memory Lane's bell.

But it will be in the name of D'onte Carroll

That just like Dr. King
the home on 340 35th Street

in Northeast D.C
will be a museum because it was
an abode I called home
belonging to the great,
legendary,
me.

Because of the name D'onte Carroll

Archbishop Carroll High School
will have a new rule
that in order to make
your name great
it is not getting famous
to see your name in lights,
but turning on your switch
called "greatness,"
recognizing that all along
your great name
was the light.

In the name of D'onte Carroll

will a block be named after me
filled with buildings to recognize
the simple fact how I shared with the world
the greatness
God placed in me.

In the name of D'onte Carroll

shall it be the key to set yet
a new detour for babes in life.
Seeking a plan to success.

In the name of D'onte Carroll

shall it show in the hit list
of your memory as
the preacher,
leader,
rebel,
poet,
lover,
father,
God-fearing
man,
husband

What's in a name?

Nothing,
a name is just a "word"
in Life's Dictionary,
the definition
is the life you live.

Ode to My Hair

To me
you are a personal element
GOD gave to me
because you possess my strength.

Not only

when I walk
 you walk
in the wind.

Not only

do you hold your position
for days at a time
when my sister puts you
in cornrows
in a straight line.

Not only

Are you there
pouring out of my head
like racing waters,

Not only do you
twist,
turn
like dancing quarters.

But you do more for me
then any other limb
on my body.

When I let you hang low
and I do a good deed
not only do you touch
my shoulders
but you pat me on the back
saying
WAY TO GO.

When my heart is weary
and I go outside in the cold
the wind blows and you
sway across my face
snatching away tears
which is really pain
translated into water
when it hits the air.

You stick to me
don't break off
just because
I make a mistake.

Thank you

for when I look
in the mirror
I see countless
duplicates of you.
Thank you
for staying true.

How to Be D'onte Carroll

Wake up every morning
and thank God
for letting me see another day.
Walk out the door with faith
in one hand,
God's Word in the other
and His hedge of protection all over me.

Listen
to how people call you everything
but a child of God.
Then look at them and smile
when they see that God still sees fit
to bless you through your mess.

Easily forgive those
who hurt you.
Wish good on those
who curse you.
Let people talk about me
as much as they please
because I talk about them
when I'm praying
down on my knees.

Look at how difficult life can get
and think to myself
I can't make it.
But let God whisper in your ear,

You can do it
you have to claim it.

Reminisce
on how God saw you through
and continue to count your blessings
and shake your head saying,
Lord I won't complain.

Try your best not to give in
to temptation.
When everybody else goes left
don't be afraid to go right.
Stand for something
when everybody else wants to stand
for nothing and fall for anything.

At the end of the day
say the prayer momma taught you
when you were five.

Now I lay me down to sleep
I pray the Lord my soul to keep

If I should die
before I wake,
I pray the Lord my soul to take.

Bless mommy,
daddy,
grandma
grandpa
Tarsha

About Me

Ra'shad
Aunt Geraldine
Uncle Mike

Amen.

Upcoming Book

17 & Married: A Memoir in the Journey to a Successful Marriage

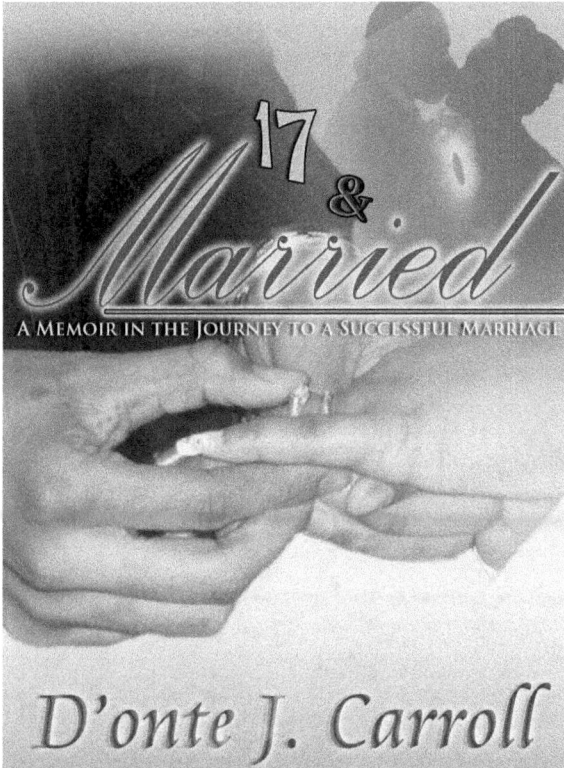

I lost my virginity to my wife when I was 17 years old, before we got married. Metaphorically speaking, I came in covenant with her before we were married. Therefore I had to fight and compete with the spirits from the different men she had been with before she was saved and we got married. Go with me as I relive my experience in my marriage, and the journey to our deliverance and how we were able to walk in our anointing as one.

Unspoken: If Walls Could Talk
...the Struggle to Deliverance

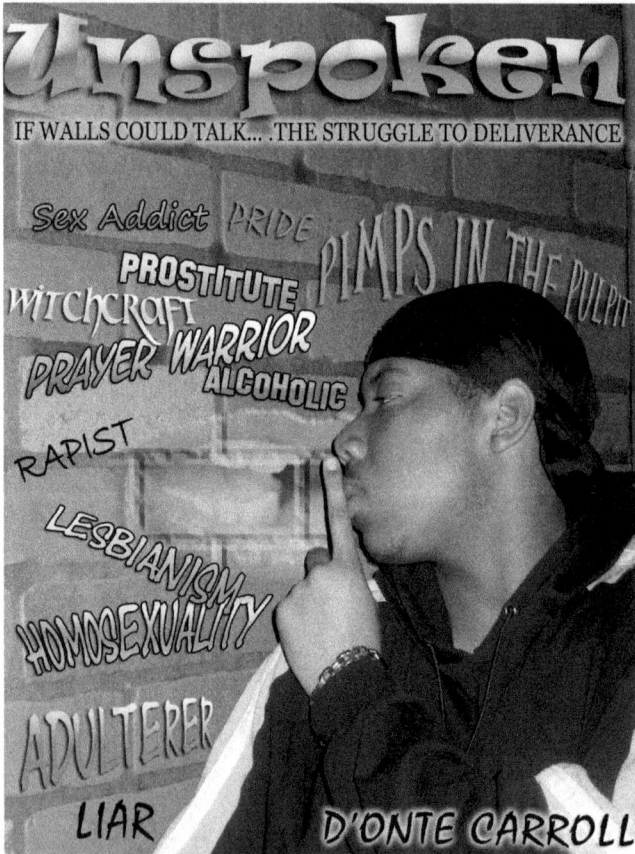

With his poetic ability, D'onte speaks for the wounded, hurting and afflicted, walking in their shoes poetically. He givies his readers a direct experience of the hardships of life and the struggle to get delivered.

About the Author

D'onte Jon Carroll was born on October 5, 1991, and raised in Southeast Washington, DC, by a single mother who always instilled in him that GOD is everything. D'onte grew up in church. It was at Christian Fellowship Baptist Church where he became aware of whom GOD is. But it was not until the age of 13 that he accepted the right hand of fellowship, was baptized, and joined the body of Christ. He officially started his walk with GOD at Varick Memorial A.M.E Zion Church in Washington, DC. Since then, he has grown into the person everyone knows and loves today.

He is the beloved husband of Abronda Carroll and the loving father of Ai'jjon, Charles, and Kenyada. He is the devoted son of Tamara Ford of Washington, DC, and Pastor Robert Johnson, Jr. of Baltimore, Maryland.

D'onte wrote his first play in the eighth grade at St. Francis Xavier Catholic School in Washington, DC. It was also there in the eighth grade where he wrote his first poem, *Black and Free*, which was chosen to be featured in the Teacher's Selection of poems from his class. From that moment on writing poetry became his life. But it was not until twelfth grade at Archbishop Carroll High School, in Washington, DC, that he developed his own style of poetry. Poetry is his mouthpiece, the translator of his inner feelings.

Currently, D'onte, is an active member of Nevi'im True Holiness Church of the Apostolic Faith in Washington, DC, under the leadership of Prophetess Buffie McIver, Pastor, and Prophet Bryan Wilson, Co-Pastor. Serving the Lord is his destiny; being a vessel is his way of putting it. Walking with the authority, power, and reverence is his way of exalting the name of the Lord. He is a saved, sanctified, Holy Ghost-filled man of GOD who knows his hope is built on nothing less than Jesus Christ and His righteousness.

Contact Information

The author is available for book signings, poetry readings, book reviews, book club discussions, and other speaking opportunities.

You may contact him by writing to:

D'onte J. Carroll
Kingdom Living Publishing
P.O. Box 660
Accokeek, MD 20607

You may also send him an email at:
carrolldonte@yahoo.com

Or connect with him on Facebook at
https://www.facebook.com/bishopcarroll

Or on Twitter at:
www.twitter.com/DonteJCarroll

For information on ordering copies of *From Pain to Poetic Justice,* please contact

Kingdom Living Publishing
10905 Livingston Road
Fort Washington, Maryland 20744
publish@kingdomlivingbooks.com
(301) 292-9010

www.ingramcontent.com/pod-product-compliance
Lightning Source LLC
LaVergne TN
LVHW051128080426
835510LV00018B/2287

* 9 780979 979835 *